Contents

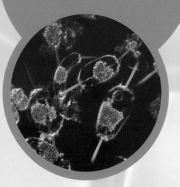

How do these tiny creatures turn into oil? Find out on page 7!

What is phantom energy? Find out on page 40!

Some words are shown in bold, **like this**. These words are explained in the glossary. You will find important information and definitions underlined, <u>like this</u>.

What are fossil fuels?

Fossil fuels include coal, oil, and natural gas. They are burned for their energy. Today, we depend on fossil fuels to provide energy for our homes, cars, and industries.

Fossil fuels form during a process that takes millions of years. In the rocks beneath Earth's surface, the remains of living things gradually change into new materials. They become high-energy **compounds** (combined substances).

The flare on top of this drilling rig is natural gas being burned off. When oil is drilled out of the ground, gas often surfaces as well.

Useful resources

Coal is burned in **power stations** to make electricity. Oil is **refined** (cleaned and separated) and turned into petrol and other fuels. These fuels power vehicles and aeroplanes. Natural gas is burned in cookers and **boilers**. People often say just "gas" when referring to natural gas.

<u>Fossil fuels are useful because of their high energy content</u>. They burn quickly and without much waste, so they are **efficient** fuels.

Oil from rocks

Petroleum is the correct name for what we usually refer to as oil. The word "petroleum" comes from the Greek words for "rock" (*petra*) and "oil" (*oleum*). Petroleum is oil that comes out of rocks!

Drawbacks of fossil fuels

Because of their many advantages, fossil fuels are widely used all over the world. Yet they are **non-renewable** (not able to be replaced). Earth's supply of fossil fuels is decreasing and will one day run out.

The use of fossil fuels is also harming the environment. <u>The burning of fossil fuels causes pollution and global climate change</u>. For these reasons, many people believe fossil fuels will eventually be replaced with **alternative** sources of energy.

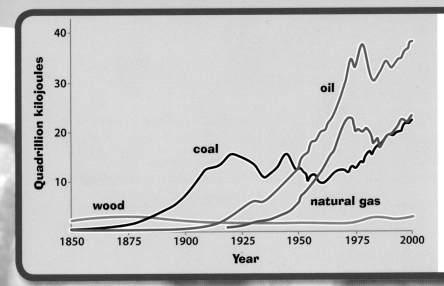

In the 19th century, wood and then coal were the world's main sources of energy. During the 20th century, oil and gas became more widely used. This chart shows how the world's use of fossil fuels has grown since 1850.

FORMING FOSSIL FUELS

The story of fossil fuels began millions of years ago in a place many millions of kilometres from Earth. That place was the Sun. Sunlight is the original energy source for fossil fuels. Fossil fuels are able to store this energy very well.

Photosynthesis

So how does the energy from sunlight turn into the energy stored in fossil fuels? First, it becomes the energy stored in living things. Plants and algae (simple life forms similar to plants) perform a process called **photosynthesis**. During photosynthesis, plants use the energy of sunlight to make glucose. Plants and algae use glucose (a type of sugar) for food.

Light energy from the Sun allows plants to split water into oxygen and hydrogen.

The plant absorbs carbon dioxide from the air.

The plant releases oxygen into the air.

During photosynthesis, the hydrogen from water joins with carbon dioxide from the air to make glucose. The carbon and hydrogen are stored in the plant, while the oxygen is released into the air.

The plant's roots gather water from the soil.

The raw materials for photosynthesis are water and **carbon dioxide**. Carbon dioxide (CO_2) is a gas that plants and algae absorb from the air.

Ancient swamps and oceans

Three hundred million years ago, Earth was a very different place from what it is today. The climate was quite hot and wet. Swamps covered much of the land. The swamps were filled with huge ferns and other kinds of plants.

When swamp plants died, their remains quickly sank and were buried. Had their remains been exposed to the oxygen in the air, they would have rotted away. But very little oxygen is present underwater, and the plants' remains did not rot away. They stored the plants' energy. Much later, the remains became coal (see page 8). The energy from the plants was then stored in the coal.

In ancient seas and oceans, a similar process buried the remains of tiny plants and animals. These remains became oil and gas (see page 10).

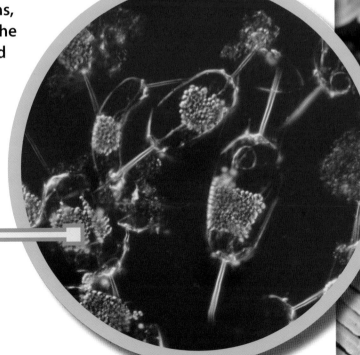

Some ancient marine plankton that formed oil and gas were similar to the microscopic plankton found in the sea today.

Coal

Coal, a type of black rock, is a solid fossil fuel. There are several types, all of which burn easily and release great amounts of energy.

How coal forms

Coal forms in several steps. First, buried plant remains break down into a moist, dark substance called peat. Next, **sediment** (settled material, such as mud) and rock bury the peat. The pressure squeezes out the water. Gradually, over millions of years, underground heat and pressure change peat into lignite. Lignite is sometimes called "brown coal". Over time, heat and pressure continue to change lignite into higher grades of coal.

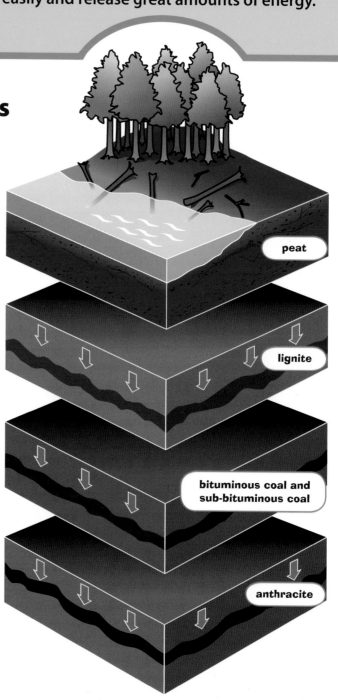

peat

lignite

bituminous coal and sub-bituminous coal

anthracite

Types of coal

ANTHRACITE is the oldest, most energy-rich coal.

BITUMINOUS COAL is used mostly to generate electricity and make coke.

SUB-BITUMINOUS COAL gives out less heat than other coals but burns more cleanly.

LIGNITE is the youngest coal with the lowest energy content.

Processing coal

Most coal is burned to produce electricity. But coal can also be processed into both a liquid and a gas. Coal gas powered the first gas lighting systems more than two hundred years ago. Liquid coal can be used as a fuel for vehicles.

Another important product from coal is a solid grey substance called coke. Coke is made by baking coal at high temperatures. It is used as a fuel or in the process of making steel.

Coal in the past

People have been mining and burning coal for its heat for many hundreds of years. Yet only since the mid-18th century has coal been used in large amounts. Before that, wood was the main fuel. In the 18th century, inventors discovered that engines and **boilers** using coal were more efficient. This was the start of a period called the **Industrial Revolution**. New machines and large factories appeared in Europe and North America. Coal provided the energy for the new industries.

The world uses about 5.6 billion tonnes (6 billion tons) of coal every year.

Oil and gas

Oil, or petroleum, is a thick, black, energy-rich liquid. It is a mixture of different **compounds** (substances with more than one kind of atom). Petroleum is also sometimes called crude oil. It must be **refined** before it can be used (see page 26).

Natural gas is a gaseous fossil fuel, which means it occurs naturally in a gas form. It consists mostly of a gas called **methane**, but it also contains propane and butane gases.

Beneath the sea bed

Deposits of petroleum and natural gas typically form together. The process is very similar to the way coal forms, but it happens in the sea instead of in swamps.

Petroleum and natural gas form from the remains of tiny sea animals and algae. The remains are buried beneath the sea bed under sand and mud. After millions of years, these layers become rock, as you can see on page 11. Over time, heat and pressure change the remains below the rock into energy-rich liquids and gases. The liquids became petroleum, and the gases became natural gas. Because gas is lighter than oil, gas deposits tend to collect above petroleum deposits. Oil and gas remained stored in the rock for centuries until people began to extract it.

Bitumen, also called asphalt, is a thick, sticky form of petroleum. In a few places, it seeps up through layers of rock to Earth's surface. The bubble you can see here comes from natural gas, which is also leaking from the ground.

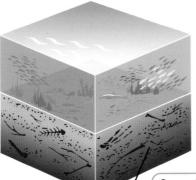
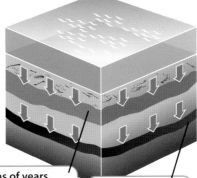

Remains of plants and animals were buried beneath sand and mud on the ocean floor.

Over millions of years, the sand and mud became rock. The remains below became more and more compressed.

Remains were changed into gas and oil that stored their energy.

Many uses

Most of the world's oil is used to make fuels. It is also used to make other products, including plastics, motor oil, wax, and road surfacing.

Natural gas is also a useful fuel. In many communities, pipelines carry gas to homes and buildings. It powers boilers, cookers, and other appliances. Compressed (squashed) natural gas can be used to power cars and lorries.

Plant and animal remains became buried under layers of sediment. Their energy was buried with them. After millions of years, the remains were changed into gas and oil that stored their energy.

Using fossil fuels: find out more on pages 24–31.

On dry land

If oil and gas form only under the sea, why do we find them under land? These deposits of oil are in rocks that formed under the sea but later became part of continents.

Fossil fuel chemistry

Just what makes up a fossil fuel? <u>Fossil fuels are made mostly of two **elements**: carbon and hydrogen</u>. **Compounds** made of only carbon and hydrogen are called **hydrocarbons**. Both coal and petroleum contain a variety of hydrocarbons. Natural gas is made mostly of **methane**, which is also a hydrocarbon.

Combustion

Burning, or **combustion**, is a common chemical reaction. A chemical reaction is the name for what happens when two or more substances combine and change. Hydrocarbons are combustible, which means they burn easily. As they burn, they join with oxygen to release two gases: **carbon dioxide** and water vapour.

Links in the chain: Find out how hydrocarbons form long chains on pages 30–31.

Coal releases an intense heat during combustion.

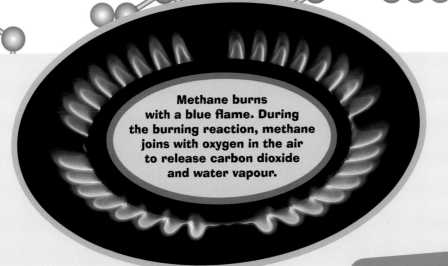

Methane burns with a blue flame. During the burning reaction, methane joins with oxygen in the air to release carbon dioxide and water vapour.

Combustion, therefore, is an opposite process to **photosynthesis**, the process used by plants. As we have already seen, photosynthesis joins carbon dioxide and water together. The energy produced is stored in fuel, such as wood and fossil fuels. <u>Burning fossil fuels restores the two compounds – carbon dioxide and water – that photosynthesis had joined together</u>. It also releases energy in the form of heat.

Smelly but safe

Natural gas has no smell in nature. This can be dangerous because leaking gas can ignite and cause an explosion. So a smelly compound called mercaptan is added to natural gas. The mercaptan lets us know when gas is leaking.

Pollution

Neither coal nor petroleum products are made only of hydrocarbons. Both contain small amounts of other compounds, including those made of nitrogen, sulphur, and other elements. When nitrogen and sulphur burn, they form chemicals that can **pollute** the atmosphere. Natural gas does not create so much **pollution**. Read more about pollution on pages 32–33.

EXTRACTING FUELS

Deposits of fossil fuels often lie deep below Earth's surface, sometimes inside a mountain or beneath the sea. They can be difficult to extract. Yet because fossil fuel deposits are so useful and valuable, people invest the money and effort needed to extract them.

Thirteen-year-old Willie Bryden (left) was working 150 metres (500 feet) below ground in a mine when this photo was taken in 1911. Coal mining was a dangerous job in those days. Mines often collapsed, killing the workers underground.

Coal mining

A mine is an area of ground that holds useful resources. Mining is a method of extracting coal and other valuable rocks and **minerals**. It involves digging near the surface or deep underground to get those resources out.

Some coal seams (deposits of coal between layers of rock) are near the surface. To extract this coal, mining companies can use **strip-mining**, which is a kind of surface mining. Layers of rock are stripped away until the coal is exposed and can be removed easily.

Deeper coal seams require shaft mining. A shaft is a deep hole dug through rock to reach the coal. At the bottom of the shaft are tunnels where miners and machines work to extract the coal.

Oil and gas wells

Oil and gas are also found deep underground. Unlike coal, they can be pumped to the surface. Workers drill a well, or deep hole, down to the deposit. When the well reaches the deposit, some of the fuel rushes to the surface. Engineers have to pump the remaining fuel up to the surface.

Offshore drilling

To extract oil and gas from under the sea, engineers set up large structures in seas and oceans. They are called offshore drilling rigs. Some rigs are platforms supported on strong legs, while others float on the water. One rig may support several wells that go off in different directions under the sea floor. Workers often stay out at sea on the platform for weeks at a time.

Once a well has been drilled, "nodding donkeys" like this one pump day and night. They bring the oil to the surface.

Red Adair (1915–2004)

A blow out happens when an oil-well suddenly gushes beyond control. Sometimes the oil catches fire. Red Adair was a fire-fighter who battled more than 2,000 fires in oilfields around the world. To stop blow outs and fight fires, he used everything from explosives to mud. Adair went to work in the oil industry in 1938 and was still fighting fires in the 1990s. He was so famous that a film was made about him, starring John Wayne.

Extraction risks

As you read this page, fossil fuels are being extracted all over the world. Usually, extraction is done safely, but sometimes there are problems and dangers. Coal mines and oil and gas wells can produce unwanted effects as well as benefits.

Pollution from mining

In strip mines, all the soil and stone above the coal is removed. This process greatly changes the environment near the mine.

The impact of coal mining reaches further away, too. Coal mining can **pollute** underground water as well as rivers and streams. It can deplete (use up) water supplies and greatly disrupt the land.

Strip mines can damage the environment for many years after the mine is exhausted (empty of coal).

Work on offshore drilling rigs keeps going night and day.

Offshore damage

Many of the world's untapped oil and gas reserves are located under the sea. In parts of the world, oil rigs are working night and day to extract those reserves. Along with oil and gas, however, offshore drilling rigs pump out other substances. Oil-wells can bring up mercury, lead, and some other **toxic** (harmful) chemicals from below the sea bed. These chemicals can escape into the sea water.

Sometimes, oil can leak into the sea water in an event called an oil spill. Although large oil spills from offshore oil rigs don't often happen, they cause terrible harm to marine life.

Oil spills: Find out more on pages 22–23

TRANSPORTING FUELS

Deposits of fossil fuels are spread unevenly around the world. <u>Fossil fuels are often found far from the places where fuels are most in demand.</u> Much money and effort is spent on transporting fossil fuels over great distances.

Where are fossil fuels?

Conditions have to be just right for fossil fuels to form. As a result, deposits of fossil fuels are found only in certain places. Half of the world's known deposits of oil are in the Middle East. More than one-third of natural gas deposits are also in that region. China and the USA have the most coal deposits.

Moving oil

An oil tanker is a ship that carries oil and oil products in huge tanks. Tankers transport about 2.3 billion tonnes (2.5 billion tons) of petroleum every year. Natural gas can also travel by tanker. To save space, the gas must be liquified (made into a liquid) before it is moved.

SHRINKING GAS
In its liquid form, natural gas takes up only 1/600th of the space of the gas!

Piping gas

A pipeline is a series of pipes that carries natural gas over long distances. Wide networks of gas pipelines cover Europe, the USA, and other parts of the world. Pipelines are also used to carry oil and even coal. The coal has to be crushed and mixed with water. Then it is dried at the other end.

Carrying coal

Most coal in the UK travels on railways. In parts of Europe, some coal travels on **barges** along rivers and canals. China produces more coal than any other nation. There, coal travels by railway and by road.

Trains take coal from the mines to the **power stations**. They can carry large amounts of coal across continents.

The Alaska Pipeline

In 1968, oil was discovered in Prudhoe Bay, just off the coast of northern Alaska in the USA. There was plenty of oil, but tankers could not safely carry it across the Arctic Ocean. To move the oil to the rest of the USA, oil companies built the Trans-Alaska Pipeline System. It is usually known as the Alaska Pipeline.

Ocean Pipelines

Some pipelines are laid on the sea bed. They bring oil from offshore oil rigs to the mainland. One pipeline connects the oilfields of the North Sea to the Shetland Islands of Scotland.

This is the start of the Alaska Pipeline in Prudhoe Bay, Alaska.

The Alaska Pipeline carries oil across Alaska for almost 1,300 kilometres (800 miles).

Alaskan challenges

The pipeline opened in 1977, connecting Prudhoe Bay with the **port** city of Valdez, Alaska. It has been carrying oil ever since. The Alaska Pipeline passes through lands of mountain ranges, streams and rivers, and many kilometres of frozen or partially frozen ground. Engineers designed the pipeline to account for all of these factors.

Oil in a pipeline must be kept hot to flow smoothly, yet high temperatures could melt the frozen ground. This is why much of the Alaskan Pipeline was built above ground. The pipeline uses thick **insulation** and a system to keep the heat inside the pipe. This protects the Alaskan **tundra** (frozen region) from melting.

Some stretches of the pipeline had to be buried. So a special refrigeration system was added to keep the ground cold.

Arctic Ocean

Trans-Alaska Pipeline System

CANADA

Pacific Ocean

Across Siberia

The Trans-Siberian pipeline carries natural gas from Siberia to western Europe. It covers a distance of 4,500 kilometres (2,800 miles).

Oil spill

On 24 March 1989, an oil tanker named the *Exxon Valdez* struck a reef off the coast of south-east Alaska, USA. Before the damage was contained, about 41.6 million litres (9 million gallons) of oil had spilled out of the ship's tanks.

Terrible damage

The spill from the *Exxon Valdez* was not the largest of all time. But because of the remote location, it was hard to respond quickly to the accident. The oil spread across 28,000 square kilometres (11,000 square miles) of ocean waters.

Safety standards

Because of *Exxon Valdez*, many countries imposed stricter safety standards on oil tankers. New tankers are built with a double **hull** – an extra layer of tough metal that contains the oil. Non-flammable gases are pumped into the oil storage containers to help prevent fires.

About 159 million litres (35 million gallons) of oil were pumped from the wrecked *Exxon Valdez* on to smaller vessels. The rest of the oil spread across the ocean surface.

In 1991, there was a war in the Persian Gulf, an oil-rich area. Soldiers from Iraq set fire to oil-wells in Kuwait. They also dumped oil from several tankers into the Persian Gulf. It was the largest oil spill in history.

The oil spill caused terrible damage. It killed huge numbers of animals. Among the dead were hundreds of thousands of seabirds, twenty-two orca whales, and countless salmon and other fish.

Cleanup

Thousands of people worked to clean up the spilled oil. It was a huge task. Yet in 2007, scientists estimated that many thousands of litres of oil remained on Alaskan beaches. They are continuing to study the long-term effects of the disaster.

OIL IN THE SEA

Less than 5 per cent of oil in the sea comes from oil spills and accidents. Most of the oil comes from waste oil that runs off the land. It comes from roads, farms, and factories. Natural seepage (oil that leaks out of the sea bed also adds more oil to the sea than accidental oil spills.

HOW WE USE FOSSIL FUELS

Products of fossil fuels are everywhere. We consume fossil fuels for heating and vehicle fuel. We use them to make electricity. Oil is processed into many different products, including the plastics that make up so many things we use in daily life.

Making electricity from coal

One of the main uses of coal is to produce electricity. Coal provides about 40 per cent of the electricity supply in the UK.

In a power station, coal is burned in a boiler. Water moves through the furnace. The heat from the burning coal changes the water into steam. The steam turns a turbine (type of engine). The spinning turbine runs a generator that makes electricity.

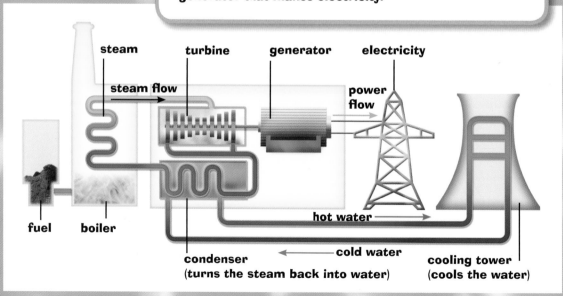

steam   turbine   generator   electricity

steam flow

power flow

fuel   boiler

hot water

condenser (turns the steam back into water)

cold water

cooling tower (cools the water)

Electricity travels through thick, **insulated** wires called power lines. The power lines connect to a network that supplies electricity to communities.

All over the world, the energy in coal is converted into electricity in **power stations**. You can think of a power station as a factory for making electricity. The energy for the power station can come from many sources, including a rushing river or natural gas. But coal is the most common source of this energy. Altogether, people use about 5.6 billion tonnes (6 billion tons) of coal every year. Almost all of it goes to making electricity.

DEALING WITH COAL POLLUTION

Coal produces more **pollution** than the other fossil fuels. Gases from burning coal rise up a chimney and are released into the **atmosphere**. Tiny black particles, called soot, are also given off. Several of these **emissions** will **pollute** land, air, and water.

Today, new technology is helping reduce that pollution. Newer **boilers** are more **efficient** and can help reduce emissions. Coal washing is a system that removes some of the pollutants from coal before it is even burned. In a different process, wet scrubbers in the chimney catch harmful gases before they are released in the air.

Petroleum products

Aside from water, petroleum may be the most useful liquid that Earth provides. Petroleum is used to make a wide variety of fuels. It also makes plastics, greases, waxes, and many other products. The first step in making any of these products is to **refine** the petroleum. It needs to be purified and separated into its parts.

One barrel of oil

A 159-litre (35-gallon) barrel of crude oil produces about 76 litres (17 gallons) of petrol and 26 litres (6 gallons) of diesel as well as many other products. The world uses about 84 million barrels of oil a day.

Refining oil

There are many different **hydrocarbons** that make up crude oil (unrefined oil straight from the ground). At an oil refinery, crude oil is separated and processed to form useful products.

At the base of tall towers, crude oil is boiled at high temperatures. The parts of the oil rise up as gases when they are heated. The lighter and smaller the hydrocarbon, the higher it rises up the towers.

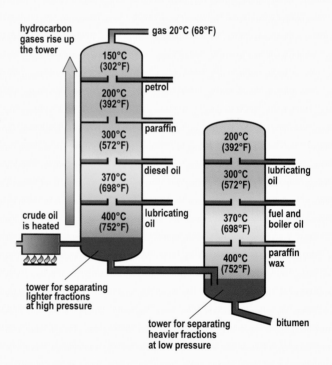

hydrocarbon gases rise up the tower

gas 20°C (68°F)

150°C (302°F)

200°C (392°F) — petrol

300°C (572°F) — paraffin

370°C (698°F) — diesel oil

400°C (752°F) — lubricating oil

crude oil is heated

tower for separating lighter fractions at high pressure

200°C (392°F)

300°C (572°F) — lubricating oil

370°C (698°F) — fuel and boiler oil

400°C (752°F) — paraffin wax

bitumen

tower for separating heavier fractions at low pressure

When the gases cool, they condense (turn back into liquids) at different levels of the towers. Trays at each level collect the separated hydrocarbons. At this stage, they are called **fractions**.

Wow!
Surprising things made from oil

balloons • bubble gum
• candles • carpets
• crayons • credit cards
• detergent • deodorant
• DVDs • explosives • food
wrappers • glue • guitar
strings • helmets • ink • life
jackets • lipstick • lotion • nail varnish
• paint • parachutes • pillows • roads • roller
skates • shoes • sunglasses • sweaters
• tyres • toys • volley-balls
• water bottles

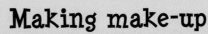

Making make-up

Oil is used to make lipstick and other types of make-up. Lipstick also contains wax, colouring, and a solvent (a substance used to dissolve other substances). To make lipstick, the ingredients are melted and mixed together. Then the mixture is poured into tubes. As it cools, the mixture hardens into a lipstick shape.

Petrol

Petrol is a mixture of hydrocarbons and other compounds. Most of this mixture is the petrol fraction produced when crude oil is refined. Other materials are added to make the petrol that vehicles use.

In many countries, a **compound** called ethanol may be added to petrol. Ethanol is made from corn and other plants. It burns well, but it does not hold as much energy as the hydrocarbons in petrol.

HANDLE WITH CARE!

Petrol is highly flammable. It must be stored in safe containers and kept away from all flames. Petrol is also very harmful if it is swallowed.

Racing cars use fuels designed for extra power and high speeds.

Fuel for racing cars

Racing cars need a lot more power than regular cars. Their engines are more powerful, but they also need special fuel. These are some of the fuels they use.

• NASCAR engines burn 98-octane unleaded petrol. **Octane** is a hydrocarbon that can handle compression (squashing) well. This makes it a good fuel for very powerful engines.

• Indy cars burn pure methanol, a fuel made from wood, coal, or natural gas. If it catches fire, the fire can be put out with water (unlike oil-based fuels).

• Top Fuel dragsters burn nitromethane, or top fuel. This explosive liquid is a mix of propane and nitric acid. Top fuel contains a huge amount of energy, but it is very dangerous.

Leaded petrol

For many years, lead, a metallic **element**, was added to petrol to improve its performance. But lead is poisonous to living things. It pollutes air, land, and groundwater. It makes people sick and damages their brains. Today, most nations have banned leaded petrol.

Plastics

The term "plastic" describes a wide variety of artificial (human-made) materials. Plastics are used to make many things in our homes and schools, such as telephones and computers. Cling film, raincoats, toys, and countless other products are made from plastic. Most plastics come from petroleum.

Plastic chemistry

Imagine linking paper loops together to form a paper chain. A similar process joins the tiny **molecules** that make up substances. A chain of small molecules makes a larger molecule called a **polymer**.

When hydrocarbon molecules join together in a chain, they can form the polymers that plastics are made of. Hydrocarbons linked in different patterns make different types of plastic.

Recycling materials conserves resources. We use so much plastic every day that we can save a lot of fossil fuels by recycling plastic.

Recycling plastic

To recycle means to reuse in one of several ways. One of those ways is to break something apart so its material can be used again. Unlike fuels made from petroleum, plastics made from petroleum can be recycled. Many communities have programmes to recycle plastic.

Some everyday plastics

Type of plastic	Used for
Acrylic	safety shields, screens, and signs
Nylon	fabrics and electronic parts
Polyethylene	rubbish bags, kitchen-ware, and toys
Polystyrene	packing material and disposable cups
Polyurethane	protective coating for wood and metal
PVC	wiring and hoses

Try it: plastics hunt

Search your classroom or home for objects made of plastic. Include the plastic parts of larger objects, such as buttons on a shirt, or the handle of a broom. Make a list to see just how much we rely on plastics every day!

Fossil fuels and the environment

People have benefitted greatly from using fossil fuels. Yet these benefits have come with many drawbacks. <u>The burning of fossil fuels **pollutes** the air and is causing global **climate** change</u>.

Smog

The term "smog" came from combining the words *smoke* and *fog*. <u>Smog is a mixture of fine particles and gases</u>. These come from the burning of fossil fuels. Coal and wood were the main sources of smog in the past. Today, most smog comes from the petrol and diesel burned in lorries and cars. Smog irritates people's eyes and lungs. This **pollution** causes health problems, too. It also harms forests, crops, and other plant life.

In cities across the world, the burning of petroleum products contributes to smog.

Acid rain can kill trees, like this one in the Blue Ridge Mountains in the USA, even if they are far away from cities and factories. The chemicals travel in the atmosphere.

SOME SMOGGY CITIES

Beijing, China

Cairo, Egypt

Hong Kong, China

Manila, Philippines

Mexico City, Mexico

Mumbai, India

New Delhi, India

Santiago, Chile

Sao Paulo, Brazil

Shanghai, China

In many cities, the high level of vehicle **emissions** creates severe smog. One type of smog is triggered by sunlight. The light reacts with fossil fuel emissions and creates harmful gases in the **atmosphere**. Because of this reaction, cities with sunny climates often have the worst smog problems.

Acid rain

When fossil fuels burn, their emissions combine with water in the atmosphere. When this water falls as rain, it is known as acid rain. Acid rain damages soil and plants. It kills fish in lakes and rivers. The acid eats into the stone used in buildings and statues.

Global climate change is causing a higher-than-usual number of severe floods.

Global climate change

Much of the pollution from fossil fuels is easy to observe. We can see smog and the results of acid rain. Other changes are harder to see.

Fossil fuels release **carbon dioxide** into the atmosphere when they burn. Over the past hundred years, people's use of fossil fuels for fuel has increased greatly. The level of carbon dioxide in the air has also increased.

<u>Rising levels of carbon dioxide in the atmosphere are causing Earth's climate to change</u>. The world is getting warmer.

THE GREENHOUSE EFFECT

Earth's atmosphere is made up of various gases that trap heat and keep Earth warm. This is known as the greenhouse effect, and the gases are called **greenhouse gases**. Carbon dioxide is a gas that traps heat especially well. Because carbon dioxide levels are rising, the greenhouse effect is becoming stronger. As a result, Earth's surface temperatures are gradually rising.

A warmer world

Rising temperatures are changing weather patterns across Earth. They are also melting **glaciers** and causing sea levels to rise. These changes can cause problems for wildlife and for people. Flooding and storms along coasts have damaged communities. Food crops suffer from bad weather or lack of water.

Right now, the world's use of fossil fuels is growing. To slow down climate change, people can reduce their use of fossil fuels for energy. Scientists are also finding ways to reduce carbon dioxide emissions.

The proposed ZeroGen power station in Queensland, Australia, will combine coal gasification with carbon capture and storage.

COAL WITHOUT CARBON DIOXIDE

Coal releases a lot of carbon dioxide when it burns. Scientists are developing several ways to reduce these emissions. One way is to capture the carbon dioxide from the chimneys of **power stations** and store it below ground. The stored carbon dioxide may be useful underground: pumping it into rock can help pump out **methane** and oil.

Another system is coal **gasification**. Using heat, coal is turned into a gas called syngas (short for synthesis gas). The syngas is burned to generate electricity. Burning syngas produces less carbon dioxide than burning coal.

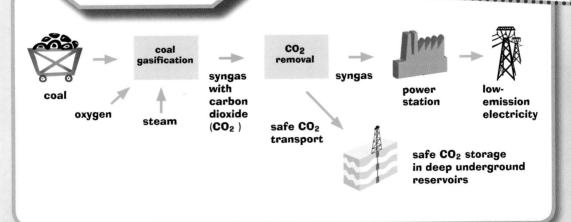

coal

oxygen

steam

coal gasification

syngas with carbon dioxide (CO_2)

safe CO_2 transport

CO_2 removal

syngas

power station

low-emission electricity

safe CO_2 storage in deep underground reservoirs

The fossil fuel supply

Fossil fuels are **non-renewable resources** – once they are used up, natural processes will not replace them for millions of years. Our use of fossil fuels, therefore, means that they will eventually run out.

Different opinions

Scientists disagree on when the world's supplies of fossil fuels will run out. Some say that we will run out of oil within the next fifty years. Others argue that supplies will hold out for much longer.

The reason for these disagreements is that no one really knows how fast we will use up fossil fuels. We also don't know the true size of Earth's supply of fossil fuels. Many lie deep underground, beneath the sea, or in remote areas of the world.

Some fossil fuel deposits are too dangerous to extract. This coal mine in Montana, USA, closed after a mining accident. It was not safe for miners to work there anymore.

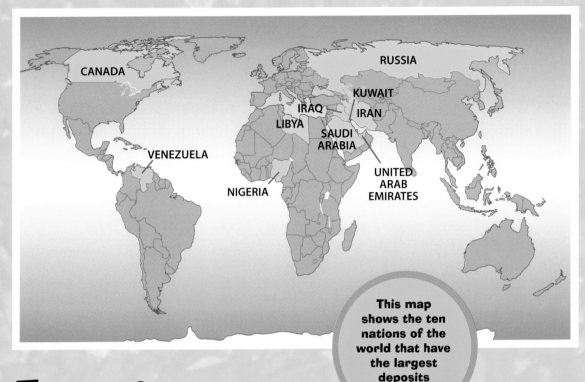

CANADA

RUSSIA

KUWAIT

IRAQ

IRAN

LIBYA

SAUDI
ARABIA

VENEZUELA

UNITED
ARAB
EMIRATES

NIGERIA

This map
shows the ten
nations of the
world that have
the largest
deposits
of oil.

Types of reserves

Deposits of coal, oil, and natural gas have been found all over the world. Some of these deposits have been used up or are almost emptied. Other deposits are being tapped today. Still others remain untapped.

A proven reserve of a fossil fuel is a deposit that has been found and measured and is possible to extract. Scientists are confident of the **data** about proven reserves.

Other deposits of fossil fuels remain to be discovered, or their sizes are unknown. They may also be too expensive or dangerous to extract. Or they may be in places where extracting them would cause too much damage to the environment. These deposits of fossil fuels are called unproven reserves.

Coal supplies

Many experts believe that coal supplies will last longer than those of oil and gas. The World Coal Institute says coal will be available for at least 150 years (compared to fewer than 50 years for oil and 65 years for gas). But these figures are based on current use, and use of coal is increasing.

Conserving fossil fuels

To conserve is to use wisely. <u>For many reasons, people are trying to conserve fossil fuels</u>. Fighting **pollution** and global warming are important reasons. Helping supplies to last longer is also very important. Saving money is yet another reason to use fossil fuels in more **efficient** ways.

Science and technology

Scientists are researching ways to conserve fossil fuels and to develop **alternative** fuels. At car companies, engineers are designing vehicles with higher fuel efficiency. Some new cars run on batteries or a combination of batteries and petrol. These vehicles are known as hybrid cars. We can already see them on our streets.

BIG DECISIONS

Governments make decisions that affect energy consumption. They can decide to build a new system of public transport instead of a new motorway. What effect do you think that would have?

Learn more about alternative fuels on pages 42-43

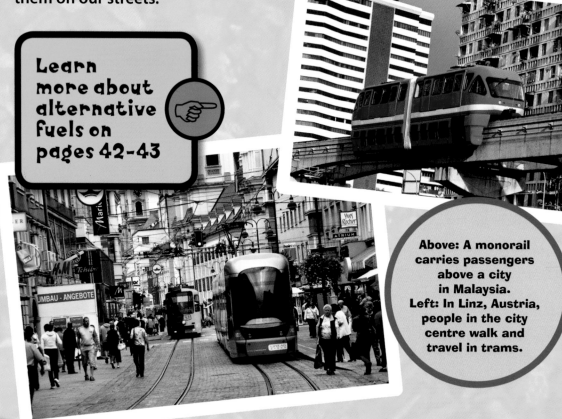

Above: A monorail carries passengers above a city in Malaysia.
Left: In Linz, Austria, people in the city centre walk and travel in trams.

Some vehicles of the future will be fueled by hydrogen instead of fossil fuels. Hydrogen can be made in fuel cells like the ones these scientists are testing. As a **renewable** fuel, hydrogen will not run out, as fossil fuels will one day.

Rising costs

When resources are in high demand, their costs go up. In 2008, the price of a barrel of oil spiked, or went up sharply. This caused the price of petrol to rise. People use less of a product when its price rises. Everywhere, people began to think about using their cars less. Many decided to buy smaller cars that use less petrol. The price went down again when demand for petrol dropped. But prices will rise over time as oil reserves get used up.

Many of the new, smaller vehicles use much less petrol than a regular car. They are popular with people who want to save money on petrol.

FOSSIL FUEL PHANTOM

It is not just governments and industries that can save energy. We can all save energy by conserving electricity at home.

Phantom load

Any device plugged into a socket is constantly drawing a small amount of energy, even when it is not in use. This energy use is known as phantom load or standby power. In Europe and the USA, phantom load accounts for between 5 and 13 per cent of the total energy use in homes!

Glowing in the dark

Take a look at the electrical appliances around your home. You will probably see several red or green lights and glowing numbers. These devices are on standby – they are still switched on even when you are not using them. Devices with a remote control, a charger, or a display have phantom loads because they are never truly "off".

Electricity eaters

All these devices can have phantom loads: TVs, stereo systems, DVD players, answering machines, fax machines, electric razors, electric toothbrushes, computers, printers, scanners, modems, routers, phone chargers, microwave ovens, and other kitchen appliances.

Fight the phantom!

You can plug several appliances into a device called a power strip. A power strip with a switch on it will turn off all the equipment at once. It stops the phantom drain of power from the appliances. Find the phantoms in your house. You could use one power strip for your computer equipment, another one for the TV and stereo, and a third one for small appliances in the kitchen.

Alternative energy

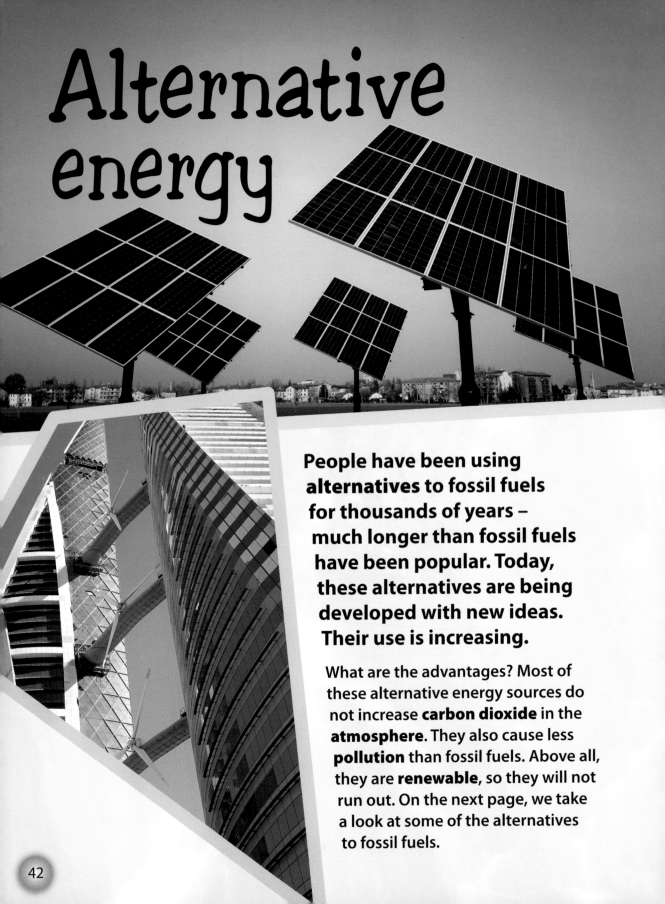

People have been using alternatives to fossil fuels for thousands of years – much longer than fossil fuels have been popular. Today, these alternatives are being developed with new ideas. Their use is increasing.

What are the advantages? Most of these alternative energy sources do not increase **carbon dioxide** in the **atmosphere**. They also cause less **pollution** than fossil fuels. Above all, they are **renewable**, so they will not run out. On the next page, we take a look at some of the alternatives to fossil fuels.

Wind power

A wind turbine is a machine that uses the wind's energy to make electricity. Wind turbines only work when the wind is blowing. Large wind farms are placed in windy spots and even out at sea.

Nuclear power

Splitting the atoms of a substance called uranium releases huge amounts of energy. The energy is turned into electricity. It can be produced in huge amounts as long as uranium supplies last.

Solar power

The energy of the Sun can be captured in solar panels to heat homes and water. Cells in some solar panels make electricity. Solar energy works well in sunny places.

Geothermal energy

Hot water and steam are brought to the surface from rocks deep underground. This heat energy can be used for heating or for making electricity.

Hydrogen fuel cells

The gas hydrogen makes a great fuel, but scientists are still working on **efficient** ways of producing it. When they do, hydrogen may power vehicles and many other things.

Biofuels

There are new ways to make fuels from plants, such as sugar-cane, corn, and wood chips. Waste from homes, farms, and factories can also be turned into biofuels.

Hydroelectricity

The power of running water is turned into electricity by **power stations** next to dams (water barriers that form reservoirs).

Fossil fuels quiz

Can you answer these key questions about fossil fuels?

1. Coal is formed from the remains of ancient _____.
  a. ocean algae
  b. animals that lived on dry land
  c. plants that grew in swamps
  d. rocks and **minerals**

2. Deposits of natural gas are often found above **deposits** of _____.
  a. coal
  b. petroleum
  c. water
  d. carbon dioxide

3. The process of separating crude oil into **fractions** involves which two steps?
  a. heating and cooling
  b. mixing and hardening
  c. drying and burning
  d. drilling and mining

4. Global **climate** change is caused mainly by the increase of _____ in the **atmosphere**.
  a. carbon dioxide
  b. water vapour
  c. hydrogen
  d. oxygen

5. Plastics differ from petrol and other fuels because they can be _____.
  a. replaced
  b. conserved
  c. burned
  d. recycled

See page 47 for answers.

Glossary

alternative different option or choice

atmosphere layer of gases that surrounds Earth and other planets

barge wide, flat-bottomed boat often used on rivers and canals for carrying heavy loads

boiler any device for burning fuel, such as boilers for home heating or the large coal-burning equipment used in power stations and factories

carbon dioxide gas composed of carbon and oxygen

climate overall weather patterns of a region over a long time

combustion chemical reaction that makes things burn, caused by combining fuel with oxygen

compound substance made of more than one kind of atom

data sets of information

deposit natural store of a fossil fuel or other minerals

efficient producing results with little waste of energy

element simple substance made of just one kind of atom

emission substance released into the air, such as gases released by the burning of fossil fuels

fraction part of something, such as the parts of crude oil that are produced from the refining process

gasification breaking down of a substance, such as coal, into gas

glacier huge piece of ice on land that is gradually moving, like a very slow river

glucose type of sugar produced by plants during the process of photosynthesis

greenhouse gas gas in the atmosphere that traps heat

hull body or frame of a ship

hydrocarbon substance that contains hydrogen and carbon

Industrial Revolution period from the middle 18th century to the late 19th century when first Europe and then North America began using machinery powered by fossil fuels

insulation protection from heat, cold, or electrical current

methane gas found in natural gas, farming waste, and other waste.

mineral element or compound that occurs naturally in Earth's surface. Rocks are made up of minerals, and many minerals are extracted from them. Fossil fuels, salt, metals, and gemstones are all minerals.

molecule group of atoms joined together

non-renewable unable to be replaced when used up

octane gas added to petrol to improve its performance in high-powered vehicles

photosynthesis process by which plants and algae make food from carbon dioxide, sunlight, and water

pollute make dirty or impure

pollution harm done to land, air, or water, usually by waste or emissions into the air

polymer large molecule made up of a chain of smaller molecules

port place along a river or coast where ships load and unload cargo

power station place where generators are used to make electricity

refine purify or clean and, in the case of crude oil, separate into useful parts

renewable able to be replaced

sediment pieces of settled material

strip mining method of surface mining that involves stripping layers of rock to expose the coal seam.

toxic poisonous or otherwise harmful

tundra large regions of the Arctic with no trees and where the deeper levels of soil remain frozen all year

Find out more

Books

Energy Sources: Fossil Fuels, Neil Morris (Smart Apple Media, 2006)

Essential Energy: Energy from Fossil Fuels, Robert Snedden (Heinemann, 2006)

Fueling the Future: Fossil Fuels and Biofuels, Elizabeth Raum, (Heinemann, 2008)

Improving Our Environment: Saving Energy, Jen Green (Wayland, 2005)

Managing Our Resources: Fossil Fuels: A Resource Our World Depends On, Ian Graham (Heinemann, 2004)

Websites

www.eia.doe.gov/kids/energyfacts/sources/non-renewable/ moreoil.html#OnKP
Energy Kids' Page--Links to Oil/Petroleum Materials
Find games and activities and more about oil from the Energy Information Administration.

science.howstuffworks.com/clean-coal.htm
What is Clean Coal Technology?
Take an in-depth look at clean coal technology and how the different methods work.

www.alliantenergykids.com/stellent2/groups/public/documents/ pub/phk_eb_ng_index.hcsp
All About Natural Gas
Learn more about how natural gas is used and how it gets to your home.

energyquest.ca.gov/index.html
Energy Quest Room
Start in the Energy Quest Room to find all the information you need about energy, how it works, and how to save it!

Quiz answers

1. c **2.** b **3.** a **4.** a **5.** d

Index